CHEVY
MUSCLE CARS

Mike Mueller

Motorbooks International
Publishers & Wholesalers

First published in 1994 by Motorbooks International Publishers & Wholesalers, PO Box 2, 729 Prospect Avenue, Osceola, WI 54020 USA

Motorbooks International books are also available at discounts in bulk quantity for industrial or sales-promotional use. For details write to Special Sales Manager at the Publisher's address

Library of Congress Cataloging-in-Publication Data

Mueller, Mike.
    Chevy muscle cars / Mike Mueller.
        p.   cm. — (Enthusiast color series)
    Includes index.
    ISBN 0-87938-864-1
    1. Chevrolet automobile—History. 2. Muscle cars—United States—History. I. Title. II. Series.
    TL215.C5M84   1994
    629.222—dc20

On the front cover: Chevy dealer Don Yenko's muscle car conversions were surely some of the most radical of the 1960s. This 1969 Yenko Camaro, belonging to Mick Price of Atwood, Illinois, came equipped with a 425 horsepower Corvette 427.
On the frontispiece: This 427 crossflag emblem was an Impala SS 427 exclusive for 1967 and 1968.
On the title page: Chevrolet's 1966 SS 396 was base-priced at $2,800. Chevelle SS 396 production for 1966 was 66,843 hardtops and 5,429 convertibles. Bob and Christa Gatchel of Clermont, Florida, own this one.
On the back cover: This 1966 Corvette sports the desirable side-mounted exhaust system and cast-aluminum knock-off wheels. Engine choices ranged from the base 250hp 327 to the outrageous 427hp 427. Ed and Diann Kuziel of Tampa, Florida, own this one.

Printed and bound in Hong Kong

Contents

Acknowledgments

The author would like to thank every car owner whose pride and joy appears within these pages. It was the cooperation, patience, and, above all, hospitality of each of them that made this book possible. In order of appearance, these lucky men and women are:

Randall and Patti Fort of New Smyrna Beach, FL, (1970 Chevelle SS 454); Roger and David Judski of Roger's Corvette Center, Maitland, FL, (1969 ZL1 and 1967 L88 Corvettes); Ervin Ray of Tavares, FL, (1966 Corvair Turbo Corsa); James Hill of West Palm Beach, FL, (1963 Nova SS convertible); Tom and Nancy Stump of North Liberty, IN, (1967 Nova SS); Dan Bennett and Jim Beckerle of Festus, MO, (1969 Nova SS 396); Steven Conti of St. Petersburg, FL, (1967 SS Camaro convertible); Paul McGuire of Melbourne, FL, (1967 Z/28 Camaro); Jim and Gina Collins of Hollywood, FL, (1967 SS 396 Camaro); Bill and Barbara Jacobsen of Silver Dollar Classic Cars, Odessa, FL, (1968 SS 396 Camaro); Mick Price of Atwood, IL, (1969 Yenko Camaro); Jim Price of La Place, IL, (1969 ZL1 Camaro); Scott Gaulter of Waukee, IA, (1964 Chevelle SS); Floyd Garrett of Fernandina Beach, FL, (1965 Z16 Chevelle SS 396); Bob and Christa Gatchel of Clermont, FL, (1966 SS 396 Chevelle); Roger Adkins of Dresden, TN, (1969 L89 SS 396 300 Deluxe sedan); Fred Knoop of Atherton, CA, (1969 COPO 427 Chevelle)—photo shoot courtesy of Roger Gibson, Roger Gibson Auto Restoration, Kelso, MO; Mick Price of Atwood, IL, (1969 Yenko Chevelle); Lukason and Sons Collection of FL, (1970 LS6 Chevelle convertible); Carl Beck of Clearwater, FL, (1970 SS 396 El Camino); Walter Cutlip of Longwood, FL, (1958 Impala convertible); Marty Locke of Lucasville, OH, (1961 Impala SS 409); Jerry Peeler of Clermont, FL, (1962 Bel Air 409); Frank Ristagno of Philadelphia, PA, (1964 Impala SS 409 convertible); Don Springer of Tampa, FL, (1967 Impala SS 427 convertible); Jim and Carol Collins of Hollywood, FL, (1969 Impala SS 427 convertible); courtesy Sullivan Chevrolet of Champaign, IL, (1970 454 Caprice); John Young of Mulberry, FL, (1954 Corvette); Ed and Diann Kuziel of Tampa, FL, (1962 Corvette); Lukason and Sons Collection of Florida (1965 396 Corvette).

Introduction
The Bow Tie Legacy

Chevrolet's fortunes took a major upswing when the "Hot One" came along in 1955. Featuring the division's first overhead-valve V-8, the tamed 1955 Chevy left Chevrolet's tired "Stovebolt" image in the dust as an unbeatable performance reputation was born almost overnight.

Chevrolet's fiberglass two-seater also received Ed Cole's OHV 265 cubic inch V-8 that same year, saving Zora Arkus-Duntov's Corvette from possible extinction. Meanwhile, thanks to Daytona Beach race car builder Smokey Yunick, 1955 Chevys had become formidable forces in NASCAR's short track division. At Yunick's urging, Chevrolet hired long-time performance product manager Vince Piggins in 1956, laying a base for a racing parts program that would help keep Chevy street performance offerings at or near the top of the heap for nearly two decades.

Chevy's small-block V-8 quickly became the hot rodder's choice, as well as a base for countless high-performance factory models. Then along came the 348 cubic inch big-block in 1958, the forerunner of the legendary 409. Introduced in 1961, the 409 roared to many victories on NHRA drag strips under Bel Air and Impala hoods.

By 1965, the full-sized 409s were displaced by lighter, high-powered intermediates. Chevrolet had introduced its A-body model, the Chevelle, for 1964, followed by the 396 cubic inch Mk IV big-block V-8 in 1965. The Mk IV transformed the Corvette into a real screamer, made the Super Sport Chevelle a crowd-pleasing success, and later did the same for the 1967 Camaro and 1968 Nova.

In 1966, the 427 cubic inch Mk IV big-block was born as an option for full-sized models and Corvettes. With Piggins' help, 427s also found their way through the Central Office Production Order (COPO) pipeline into Camaros and Chevelles three years later, despite GM's 400 cubic inch limit for intermediates and

Borrowing the lightweight, stamped steel, ball-stud rocker arm design created by Pontiac engineers, Chevrolet's 265 cubic inch overhead-valve V-8 was a high-winding powerplant with loads of potential. Introduced in 1955, the first in a long line of Chevy small-block V-8s, it was rated at 180 horsepower with a four-barrel carb and dual exhausts.

pony cars. (GM had passed an anti-racing edict in 1963 and was trying to downplay performance.) The ZL1 aluminum 427 Camaro and L72 cast-iron 427 Chevelle, both limited edition COPO creations built for 1969, stand among Chevrolet's hottest products, surpassed only by the 1967–1969 L88 aluminum head 427 Corvettes and their more exotic 1969 ZL1 427 siblings—all impressive, but well beyond the average customer's reach.

On a more realistic scale, 1970 was the pinnacle year for Chevrolet performance. This was due in no small part to the lifting of the 400 cubic inch limit for its smaller model lines and the resulting creation of the SS 454 Chevelle. In 450 horsepower LS6 trim, the 1970 SS 454 may well have represented Detroit's strongest regular-production muscle car, with low 13-second quarter-mile runs possible right off the truck.

But by 1971, tightening federal emissions standards had brought on drastically lowered

Two of Chevrolet's most powerful offerings, the 1967 L88 (in back) and 1969 ZL1 Corvettes. Both cars were drastically underrated at 430 horsepower, with more than 500 horses at the ready from both the aluminum head L88 and all-aluminum ZL1 427 big-block V-8s. While a mere twenty L88 Corvettes were built for 1967, only two ZL1s were produced two years later.

compression ratios and stifling pollution control equipment. Detroit's muscle car era came to an end in a morass of rising insurance rates and escalating safety and environmental concerns. Chevrolet's street performance legacy basically went dormant after 1972, re-emerging less than a decade later when technology began to meet the demands of the modern performance market.

Perhaps Detroit's most popular muscle car, Chevrolet's Super Sport Chevelle reached the pinnacle in SS 454 form for 1970. In base trim, the SS 454 featured the 360 horsepower LS5 454 cubic inch big-block. The king of the hill, however, was the LS6, which pumped out 450 horsepower worth of mid-sized muscle.

Chapter 1

Big Guns
Full-Sized Flyers from 409 to 454

In the beginning—before Camaros, before Chevelles, before Sting Rays—there was the 409, Chevrolet's legendary, lyrical, performance powerplant. When the 409 was introduced in 1961, big cubes in big cars represented the only way to fly as Detroit's muscle car wars were just beginning to heat up. For Chevy, escalation had begun in 1958, the year engineers transformed the 348 "W-head" truck engine into the first beefed-up Bow Tie big-block V-8. With triple two-barrel carbs, the 348 initially maxed out at 315 horsepower, but by 1961 it was producing 350 horses.

That same year, Chevy engineers upped the ante again, recasting the W-head V-8's block to make room for 409 cubic inches. And to showcase the new 360 horsepower 409, Chevrolet introduced the Impala Super Sport, a classy hardtop that would reign supreme as one of the 1960s top full-sized performers.

In typical fashion, the 409 progressed up the performance ladder each year, receiving two four-barrel carbs in 1962 to raise output to 409 horsepower, then reaching a maximum of 425 horsepower in 1963. But by 1965, the coming of the 396 cubic inch Mk IV big-block V-8 spelled the end for the antiquated 409, which had dropped to 400 horses in top tune. Production of 400- and 340-horsepower 409s for 1965 reached 2,828, bringing the five-year total to 43,755.

Introduced midyear in 1965, the 396 cubic inch big-block helped diehards forget all about the 409. Offered in two forms, 325- and 425-horsepower, the 396 Mk IV was an instant suc-

Once Chevrolets began putting on considerable weight in the late 1950s, engineers responded with more horsepower and torque. Beginning in 1958, the additional power came courtesy of the 348 cubic inch "W-head" V-8. Also introduced in 1958, Chevy's decked-out Impala weighed as much as 300lb more than the previous year's topliner, the 1957 Bel Air.

cess, reaching sales of nearly 60,000 for the year. In 1966, another Mk IV big-block was introduced as the 396 was bored and stroked to 427 cubic inches, identical to the Mk IV's forefather, the Mk II "Mystery Motor" that had first appeared for NASCAR action at Daytona in February 1963. Although maximum 427 output, at 425 horses, was the same as the 396, that power was achieved at 800 less rpm.

Chevrolet's top Mk IV big-block was an option for all full-sized 1966 models and became the star of the Impala Super Sport line in 1967 with the arrival of the SS 427. Offered along with the standard Impala SS, the SS 427 reappeared in 1968, and again in 1969, as the last of the full-sized Super Sports. Although the SS imagery was gone, buyers of full-sized Chevys in 1970 could still order the 390 horsepower 454, and in 1971 the detuned 365 horsepower 454 remained available. By then, however, luxury was the main selling point as big car performance had long since faded away.

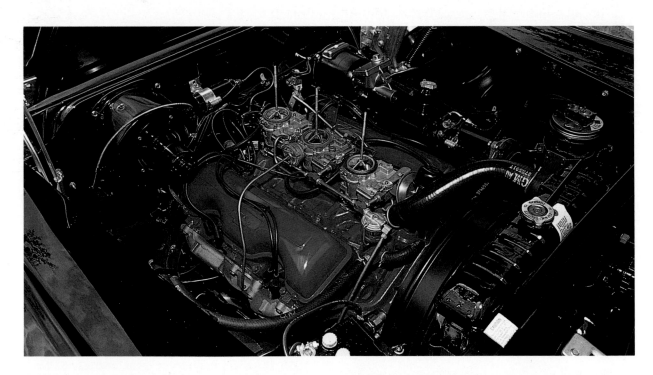

The 348 was originally designed for truck duty and is easily recognized by its valve covers, which resemble a *W* or an *M* depending on your perspective. With one four-barrel carburetor and 9.5:1 compression, Chevy's first Turbo-Thrust 348 was rated at 250 horsepower. Exchanging the four-barrel for three Rochester two-barrels upped output to 280 horsepower. At the top was the maximum performance Super Turbo-Thrust 348 featuring a solid-lifter Duntov cam, 11:1 compression, and the same three Rochesters; output was 315 horses.

Introduced shortly after the famed 409 made the performance scene early in 1961, the Impala Super Sport represented icing on the cake. Chevrolet's Super Sport kit, an optional package for the Impala line (originally, brochures even advertised a stillborn four-door model), was rolled out to showcase the new 409, though the venerable 348 was an available 1961 SS power source. Exterior SS treatment included spinner wheel covers and "SS" badges on the rear quarters and deck lid. Only 453 1961 Impala Super Sports were built; 409 production for 1961 was a mere 142 units.

Although nearly identical in outward appearance to its 348 forerunner, the 1961 409 was quite different internally with a beefier block, forged aluminum pistons, and a more aggressive solid-lifter cam. Compression was 11.25:1; output was 360 horsepower at 5800rpm. Fuel/air was supplied by a Carter four-barrel on an aluminum intake that was painted in early cars despite the fact that the paint quickly peeled. Dressed up with chrome by many owners, the 1961 409 was originally delivered with painted valve covers and air cleaners. This 409 is incorrectly equipped with a 348 single-snorkel air cleaner; 1961 409s had dual-snorkel units.

Left
Super Sport interior modifications included a sport steering wheel with a column-mounted 7000rpm tachometer, a Corvette-style grab bar on the passenger side of the dash, and a bright floor plate housing the shifter in four-speed cars.

Although the preferred 409 application for the sake of image was the Super Sport Impala, drag racers were better off choosing the lighter, less expensive Bel Air "bubbletop" coupe. Nineteen sixty-two Bel Airs—like this 409 horsepower dual-quad 409 version—were a common sight in NHRA winners' circles.

In 1962, revised heads and a hotter cam upped 409 output to 380 horsepower with a single four-barrel carburetor. Priced at $428, the 380 horsepower 409 was only the beginning. Sixty dollars more added twin Carter AFBs, increasing the 409's advertised maximum rating to 409 horsepower at 6000rpm. Painted valve covers were the norm in 1962; in 1963 chrome dress-up became standard 409 fare. Total production of 1962 409s was 15,019.

S he's real fine, my 409.
—The Beach Boys, *409*

The most outrageous 409 was the Z11 factory
drag package, which first appeared in very
limited numbers in late 1962 for NHRA A/FX
competition. Z11 components included
replacement heads, pistons, and cam for the 409
horsepower 409, along with a special two-piece
intake manifold. Also included were aluminum
fenders, inner fenders, and hood. In 1963,
aluminum front and rear bumpers were added to
the Z11 option group, as was a special 409
stroked to 427 cubic inches. The 1963 Z11 was
easily identified by its NASCAR-style cowl plenum
air cleaner setup. Laughably underrated at 430
horsepower, the Z11's actual output was more
than 500 horses.

Right
The distinctive anodized aluminum bodyside
trim pieces with their swirl pattern had become a
Super Sport trademark in 1962, but truly stood
out running down the bodyside of a 1964 Impala
SS. Easily the most popular among Detroit's sporty
full-sized crowd, the 1964 Super Sport attracted
185,325 buyers. This 409-equipped 1964 SS
convertible features the optional wire wheel
covers in place of the familiar flat Super Sport
spinners.

In 1963 and 1964, Chevrolet offered three different 409s. At the top was the dual-quad 425 horsepower version, RPO L80. Next down the ladder was the single-carb 400 horsepower L31. Tamest of the bunch, and the only 409 available with an automatic transmission, was the 340 horsepower L33. This 1964 L33 V-8 was one of 8,864 409s built for 1964, down from a high of 16,902 the previous year.

Right
New for 1967 was a Super Sport package built specifically around an engine option: the Impala SS 427. Powered by the 385 horsepower 427, the 1967 SS 427 was offered in hardtop or convertible form and featured heavy-duty suspension, a special domed hood, a blacked-out rear cove panel with "SS 427" identification, and unique "SS 427" crossflags on the front fenders. Only 2,124 of these high-priced, high-powered showboats were built.

Included with the SS 427 package, and optional on other 1967 Chevys, the L36 427 produced a maximum 385 horses at 5200rpm; maximum torque was 460lb-ft at 3400rpm. Compression was 10.25:1. Even with all that torque, throwing a two-ton 1967 Impala around was no easy task. According to *Car Life*, a 1967 SS 427 went 0–60mph in 8.4 seconds; quarter-mile time was 15.75 seconds at 86.5mph.

Right
The last Impala Super Sport came in 1969, and it went out with a bang as the SS 427 was the only model offered. Absent was a special domed hood (used in 1967) and fender "gills" (a 1968 SS 427 feature); in their place were large "SS" fender badges and a custom grille. Nearly unnoticeable "427" badges were incorporated with the front fender marker lights. Production for the last of the three SS 427 models was 2,455.

Listed under RPO Z24, the SS 427 package for 1969 included this 390 horsepower 427 Turbo-Jet. Mildly modified cylinder heads and pistons made for a five horsepower increase compared to the 1967 and 1968 L36s. Maximum torque remained the same at 460lb-ft, but came 2000rpm higher at 3600 revs.

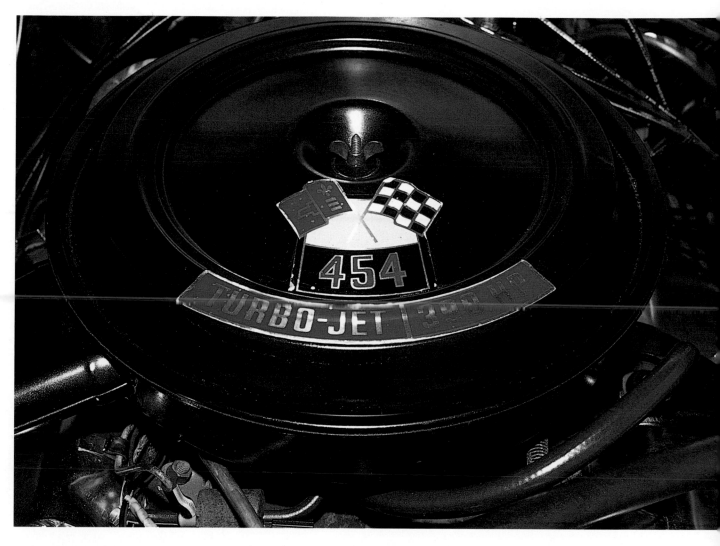

As standard equipment under an SS 454 Chevelle's bulging hood, the LS5 454 was rated at 365 horsepower. In full-sized applications, Chevy's LS5 carried the Corvette's 390 horsepower output rating. At 500lb-ft, torque output was the same for all LS5 applications, as were 10.25:1 pistons.

*S*S 427: just the ticket for the sporting man who likes some room to move around in.

—1967 Chevrolet advertisement

By 1970, the Super Sports were gone but an Impala or Caprice customer in search of full-sized performance could still check off Chevy's biggest big-blocks as an option. This Caprice sport coupe is powered by the LS5 454. Along with all that big-block brute force, this Caprice also features many of the comforts of home, from power door locks, seats, and windows, to a tilt wheel and AM/FM stereo. Performance options include the 15in Rally wheels, F40 sport suspension, and G80 positraction rear end.

Chapter 2

Mighty Mites
Corvairs and Novas

Chevrolet performance models came in all shapes and sizes, not the least of which were the compact Corvairs and Chevy IIs. Introduced in 1960 and 1962, respectively, both models were initially offered as budget-minded competition aimed at the foreign compacts that had gained a foothold in the American market in the late 1950s.

Many customers, however, looked at the Corvair as a Euro-style sportster. In 1961, 42.5 percent chose the optional bucket seats, followed by 64.6 percent in 1962 and 80.5 percent in 1963. By 1965, the only body style available was a sporty hardtop roofline offered in both four- and two-door form. Enhancing the sporty image were various optional performance packages, beginning in 1962 with heavy-duty, sintered-iron brakes, a positraction transaxle, and special handling equipment.

Big news for 1962 was the Monza Spyder, a true performance Corvair powered by a turbocharged version of Chevrolet's air-cooled, 145 cubic inch six-cylinder opposed engine. With 10lb of boost, the turbo upped the pancake six's output to an impressive 150 horsepower. Both convertible and coupe Spyders were produced for three years, though the turbo option carried on after the Spyder's demise. For 1965 and 1966, the turbocharged Corvair Corsa six-cylinder displaced 164 cubic inches and was rated at a healthy 180 horsepower.

The performance angle was initially a bit tougher to come by for Chevy II buyers. No ifs, ands, or buts about it, the first Chevy II was a 100 percent budget buggy with power coming

Along with being the last year for the Chevy II designation, 1968 was also the first year for the SS 396 Nova, which was offered through 1970. Almost identical to its 1968 forerunner, this 1969 SS 396 Nova features optional Rally wheels. SS 396 exterior trim included the blacked-out grille with "SS" badge and "396" identification in the front marker lights.

Although the Monza Spyder had been discontinued after 1964, a turbocharged Corvair was still available in 1965 and 1966. Available only on Corsa hardtops like this 1966, the turbocharger option featured no external imagery—like the earlier Spyders—save for a small, round emblem on the deck lid. The chin spoiler was a standard Corsa feature in 1966.

from either a frugal 90 horsepower 153 cubic inch four-cylinder or a 120 horsepower 194 cubic inch six. Although a V-8 swap was made available midyear as a dealer option, its price tag ran as high as 75 percent of a 1962 Nova sports coupe's sticker.

Performance imagery came along in 1963 with the Super Sport option. First offered on Impalas in 1961, the SS package for Novas included special trim and wheel covers, bucket seats, instrumentation, and a deluxe steering wheel. True performance debuted in 1964 with the first optional Chevy II V-8, the 195 horsepower 283. Two years later, Chevrolet's little Nova joined super car ranks with the addition of the L79 option, a 350 horsepower 327 that transformed a Chevy II into a polite 15.10 second quarter-mile contender.

Small-blocks were the limit for Chevy II customers until 1968, when the 396 big-block

became available early in the model run. Standard power for the 1968 Nova SS 396 came from a somewhat mild 350 horsepower big-block, with a serious 375-horse version also listed. According to *Popular Hot Rodding*, a 375 horsepower SS 396 Nova could run the quarter in 13.85 seconds, topping out at 104mph. SS 396 Novas were dropped after 1970, leaving the 270 horsepower 350 cubic inch small-block as the top power choice in 1971.

A revised turbocharger and an increase in displacement from 145 cubic inches to 164 cubic inches helped pump up output from the Spyder's 150 horsepower to 180 horsepower in 1965. Here, a Saginaw four-speed sends this 1966 turbo six's torque through a 3.55:1 positraction transaxle.

With bucket seats, a four-speed stick, and an attractive dash layout featuring full instrumentation, a turbocharged 1966 Corsa Corvair offered as much sporty imagery inside as it did performance beneath its rear deck lid.

Right
A Nova SS convertible was offered only in 1963, the same year the Super Sport equipment was first made available to Chevy II buyers. Six-cylinder power was as hot as it got for the 1963 Nova SS, though an ultra-expensive (roughly $1500 or more) dealer-option V-8 swap was listed. Super Sport Nova production for 1963 reached 42,432, with no breakdown given for sports coupe or convertible. The 1963 Nova Super Sport's exterior features included SS wheel covers (from the 1963 Impala Super Sport), special beltline trim, "Nova SS" emblems on the tail and rear quarters, and a silver rear coverpanel.

Priced at $161, the Super Sport option for the 1963 Chevy II Nova added bucket seats, a deluxe sport steering wheel, and a four-gauge (oil, ammeter, temperature, fuel) instrument cluster. A bright molding spanned the center of the dash, and a "Nova SS" emblem was added to the glovebox. Powerglide-equipped Nova Super Sports got a floor shifter with an attractive chrome plate (all three-speed cars included column shifts).

Right
The Chevy II's body was restyled in 1966, while the Nova SS was recharged with the addition of the optional L79 327 V-8. Featuring a Holley carburetor, 11:1 compression, and big-valve heads, the L79 produced 350 horsepower. Sadly, the L79 option was discontinued for 1967, the year in which front disc brakes were first offered. This yellow 1967 Nova SS shows off its attractive, slotted Rally wheels, which were included when front discs were ordered.

Nova SS: a quick looking coupe you can order with the toughest block on the block.

—1968 Chevrolet advertisement

Like Chevelle SS 396s, a big-block Nova Super Sport featured a blacked-out rear cove panel with an "SS" badge in the center. An "SS" steering wheel was also included inside. This gold 1969 SS 396 Nova is one of 5,262 equipped with the 375 horsepower big-block; another 1,947 were built with the 350 horsepower 396. Total 1969 Nova Super Sport production, including small-blocks, was 17,654.

This innocuous badge incorporated into the side-marker light on both front fenders was the only clue to the presence of a 1969 SS 396 Nova. Priced at $280 above the cost of a Nova coupe, the standard Super Sport featured a 350 cubic inch small-block V-8. Price for the 350 horsepower SS 396 package was $464; the 375 horsepower version cost $596.

Left
Fitted with 11:1 compression, a big Holley four-barrel on an aluminum intake, free-breathing heads, and solid lifters, the 375 horsepower 396 was a no-nonsense muscular powerplant, "a very serious engine to stuff into an unsuspecting Chevy II," according to *Car and Driver*. Performance was equally serious at 14.5 seconds through the quarter-mile. Top speed was an estimated 121mph.

Chapter 3

Mid-Sized Muscle
From Chevelle to Monte Carlo

Chevrolet general manager Semon E. "Bunkie" Knudsen introduced the Chevelle in August 1964 to rave reviews, both from the press and from the car-buying public. Chevy's popular new A-body was smart looking, easy to handle, and offered ample comfort. Performance potential was also present, though it would be more than a year before that was fully tapped.

Initially, the best a performance-minded Chevelle customer could do was to add the $162 Super Sport equipment group, which featured more sporty flair than anything else. Even mundane six-cylinder power was a Super Sport option in 1964 and 1965; but midway through the 1964 model year, the 327 cubic inch small-block V-8 was made available. Then in 1965 the truly hot 350 horsepower L79 327 appeared as an option.

Really big news came in February 1965 when Knudsen again did the introductory honors, this time for Chevy's first SS 396 Chevelle, the fabled 1965 Z16. The limited edition Z16 was powered by a 375 horsepower 396 mated to a Muncie four-speed and loaded with a host of options that ran its bottom line up to about $4,200. Publicity was the driving force behind the Z16's existence. Only 201 examples were built—200 hardtops and one mysterious convertible. The lone drop-top was built as an executive car. It was eventually sold off, and its final fate remains unknown to date.

Credit for inspiring COPO 9562 Chevelle production basically goes to Don Yenko, who ordered ninety-nine 427-equipped A-bodies for his Chevy dealership in Canonsburg, Pennsylvania. When the Chevelles arrived, they were converted into Yenko Super Cars. Graphics and badges identical to the Yenko Camaro's were added, as were optional Atlas five-spoke mags on request. Of the ninety-nine 1969 Yenko Chevelle SCs built, twenty-two were four-speed cars, and seventy-seven were equipped with Turbo-Hydramatics, like this Fathom Green example.

After 1965, Chev elle Super Sports came only with the 396 cubic inch Mk IV V-8—no more small-blocks or six-cylinders. Offered in more affordable, less plush form, the base 1966 SS 396 Chevelle relied on a 325 horsepower 396, with 360- and 375-horse big-blocks available at extra cost. Carrying a price tag right around $3,000, Chevrolet's SS 396 quickly raced to the forefront of Detroit's super car scene.

In 1969, the SS 396 package was improved greatly with the addition of front disc brakes and the F41 sport suspension group as standard equipment. As for power options, new for 1969 was the aluminum head L89 option for the L78 375 horsepower 396, features that didn't change output on the street, but saved considerable weight at the track. Also new was the COPO 9562 Chevelle, a rare 427-powered variant created in order to supply Don Yenko

With its 115in wheelbase (identical to the 1955 Chevy), super clean slab sides, and scalloped rear wheel openings, Chevrolet's 1964 Chevelle clearly picked up where the famed "Hot One" had left off. The crossflag fender emblem on this 1964 Chevelle Super Sport indicates the presence of the optional 327 cubic inch V-8, introduced in three power levels midway through the model year. The L30 327 was rated at 250 horsepower, while the L74 put out 300 horses. At the top was the mysterious 365 horsepower L76 Corvette 327, a true performance powerplant that was officially offered then quickly cancelled before true production got underway. No more than a handful were built; this 1964 SS was assembled to L76 specs by its owner to demonstrate an ultra-rare breed.

The Super Sport option group for the 1964 Chevelle was identified by special trim on the upper body line, rockers, and wheel openings; SS wheel covers; and "SS" badges on the rear quarters and back cove panel. Super Sport Chevelle hardtop production for 1964 was 57,445 for V-8 cars and 8,224 for six-cylinders. Standard power for a V-8 Chevelle SS in 1964 was a 195 horsepower 283 cubic inch small-block.

with base models for his Yenko Super Car transformations.

Once GM's 400 cubic inch limit for intermediates was lifted after 1969, the sky became the limit. Chevy's SS 396 remained available—with actual displacement at 402 cubic inches. But the top dog was the SS 454, available in two forms—the 360 horsepower LS5 and the

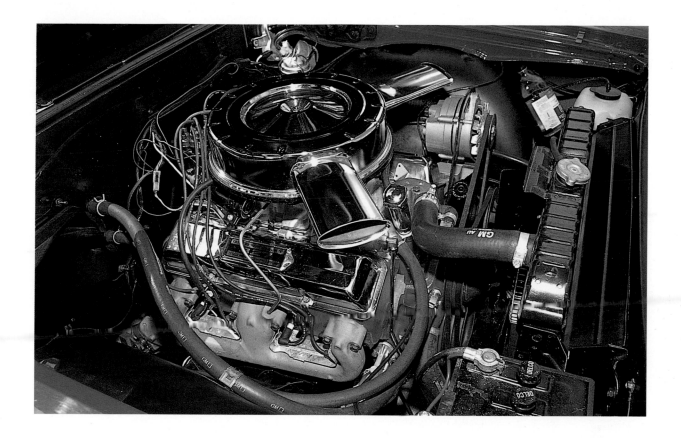

450 horsepower LS6. The latter engine's greater horsepower was attributable in part to closed chamber heads with bigger valves, 11.25:1 compression, a 0.520in lift cam, and a 780cfm Holley four-barrel. Able to leap tall buildings in a single bound, the 13-second LS6 ranks as one of the greatest super cars of all time. But the LS6 legend was short-lived. Although initially offered again, this time in 425 horsepower tune, the LS6 454 Chevelle failed to reappear in 1971, a victim of skyrocketing insurance rates, growing safety concerns, and impinging emissions standards.

By 1971, the Chevelle SS was again made available, though now with small-block power

Reportedly the A-body chassis made it difficult to equip the 365 horsepower L76 327 with large enough exhaust manifolds, which helped kill the project before it ever got off the ground. A certified street killer, the L76 small-block featured a solid-lifter "special performance cam," 11:1 compression, a big four-barrel carb on an aluminum intake, and a dual-snorkel air cleaner. According to rumors, a prototype L76 Chevelle ran 0–60mph in six seconds.

for the first time since 1965. The SS 454 managed to stick around through 1972, still a force to be reckoned with, but only a mere shadow of its former self. After 1973, all that remained were memories.

Z16 Chevelles differed from 1965 small-block Super Sports in back, where the "Malibu SS" rear quarter script was removed (reinstalled up front) and the tail dechromed. Less ornate 300 series taillights were installed, as was a blacked-out rear cove panel and a "Malibu SS 396" deck lid badge. A base 1965 V-8 Chevelle SS was priced at $2,600. Throw in the $1,501.05 for RPO Z16, along with the cost of a few other options, and the overall sticker got heavy in a hurry.

Left
A limited edition, fully loaded teaser for the big-block Chevelle bloodline to come, 1965's Z16 was both high-priced and high-powered. All 201 Z16s were equipped with the 375 horsepower 396 cubic inch Mk IV V-8 backed by a Muncie M20 four-speed with 2.56:1 low —an automatic transmission wasn't available. Gold-line rubber with simulated mag-style wheel covers, a blacked-out grille, "396 Turbo-Jet" fender emblems, and the transplanted "Malibu SS" badge (from the rear quarters to the front fenders) were all included in the Z16 deal.

49

Appearing first in 427 cubic inch "Mystery Motor" form at the Daytona 500 in February 1963, Chevrolet's Mk IV big-block V-8, RPO L37, was introduced for street duty in 1965. The 396 cubic inch mill became an option for Corvettes and full-sized models and was made the heart of RPO Z16. Under Z16 Chevelle hoods, the L37 396 was rated at 375 horsepower. Unlike the 425 horsepower Corvette 396, which used a solid-lifter cam, the Chevelle big-block relied on hydraulic lifters. Other L37 features included a Holley four-barrel, aluminum intake, and 11:1 extruded aluminum pistons.

Standard 1965 Z16 interior included bucket seats, front and rear seatbelts, AM/FM four-speaker stereo, a 160mph speedometer, 6000rpm tach, oil gauge, and dash-mounted clock. Optional equipment seen here includes power windows and a sport steering wheel with simulated woodgrain rim. As with exterior paint, Z16 interior color choices numbered only three: black, white and red, with red not offered with the Crocus Yellow paint. Regal Red and Tuxedo Black finishes were the other two exterior choices.

Chevelle SS396. And the SS doesn't stand for "Standing Still."

—1967 Chevrolet advertisement

This cowl plenum intake system was offered over dealers' parts counters for 1966 Chevelle SS 396s (the setup had first appeared on the rare 1963 Z11 A/FX Impala), though it would become better known as a Z/28 Camaro option the following year. A rare Chevelle feature, this NASCAR-style induction setup sits atop a 375 horsepower L78 396, of which 3,099 found their way under SS 396 hoods in 1966. Also featured on this car is the M22 Muncie "Rock Crusher" four-speed, one of only eighteen ordered by 1966 SS 396 buyers.

Right
For one year only, the SS 396 package, RPO Z25, was offered on both the top-line Malibu hardtops and convertibles, and on the lower priced 300 series models, making an SS 396 sedan possible in 1969. No breakdowns are available, but this Hugger Orange SS 396 300 Deluxe sedan is certainly a rare bird, especially when you consider it's powered by an aluminum-head L89 396. All 1969 SS 396s, regardless of body style or model line, came with 14x7in five-spoke sport wheels.

Aimed at racers who preferred cutting weight wherever possible, RPO L89 added a pair of lightweight aluminum cylinder heads to the 375 horsepower L78 396. Output for the L89/L78 big-block V-8 remained the same. Only 400 L89 Super Sport Chevelles were built for 1969, with estimates claiming as many as six of the aluminum-head 396s installed in SS 396 300 Deluxe sedans.

The 425 horsepower L72 427 carried no identification under a COPO Chevelle's hood, leaving some believing it was just another 396. Much hotter than even the 375 horsepower L78, the L72 featured 11:1 compression, a 0.520in lift, solid-lifter cam, and an 800cfm Holley four-barrel carb. COPO Chevelles turned low 13 second quarter-miles. Although exact production figures aren't available, it is known that Chevrolet built ninety-six L72 V-8s for COPO Chevelles with Turbo-Hydramatics (code MP) and another 277 425 horsepower 427s for four-speed COPO 9562 applications. The 373 total represents engines built, not cars assembled.

Right
Somewhat of a mystery still today, the 1969 COPO 9562 Chevelle was a little-known variation on the big-block A-body theme. Like the COPO Camaros, this Chevelle was equipped with the L72 427 Corvette V-8. COPO Chevelles featured the SS 396's hood, exhaust extensions, grille, and blacked-out tail treatment (with "SS 396" badges removed front and rear), but the car wasn't a Super Sport. Both the SS 396 bodyside stripes and Rally wheels were optional, with the Rallys being 15x7in units; optional Malibu Rally rims in 1969 were fourteen-inchers, while all SS 396s rolled on their own exclusive 14x7in five-spoke wheels.

The L72 427 under Yenko Chevelle hoods was rated at 450 horsepower. A set of Doug Thorley headers was offered as a Yenko option, but few were ordered. According to *Super Stock & Drag Illustrated's* Ro McGonegal, a 1969 Yenko Chevelle could trip the lights at the far end of the quarter-mile in 13.31 seconds at 108mph—on street tires.

Right
Considered by many as the king of the muscle car hill, the 1970 LS6 SS 454 Chevelle ranked easily among Detroit's quickest performance machines, achieving low 13-second quarter-miles with relative ease. Breaking into the 12-second bracket was also possible with a few modifications. This LS6 convertible, looking somewhat plain without the typical cowl induction hood and optional striping, is one of about twenty built (some production estimates also go as high as seventy-five). Total 1970 LS6 production—convertible, hardtop, and El Camino—was 4,475.

Left
Car Life claimed the 450 horsepower LS6 454 was "the best super car engine ever released by General Motors." Free-breathing, closed-chamber heads; 11.25:1 compression; a 0.520in lift, solid-lifter cam; and a 780cfm Holley four-barrel atop a low-rise aluminum manifold were among the LS6's supporting cast. Torque output was an impressive 500lb-ft at 4000rpm. The twin-snorkel air cleaner shown here is one of three types used on LS6 454 Chevelles.

Previous pages
From 1966 on, El Camino models could be equipped with nearly all features common to Chevelle Super Sports—including the 396 big-block V-8. It wasn't until 1968, however, that they actually wore Super Sport badges . For 1968 only, the SS 396 El Camino was a separate model in itself. From 1969 to 1970, the SS 396 package, RPO Z25, was listed as an option for El Caminos, as it was in Chevelle ranks. In 1971, the SS 396's RPO number changed to Z15. This 1970 SS 396 El Camino is equipped with the popular optional cowl induction hood and 350 horsepower big-block.

Above
Joining Chevrolet's A-body ranks in 1970 was the Monte Carlo, a personal luxury car that could also be outfitted in Super Sport garb. Offered in both 1970 and 1971, the SS 454 Monte Carlo was a classy torque monster fit with heavy-duty suspension. Exterior identification consisted only of two small "SS 454" rocker badges and twin chrome exhaust extensions in back. This 1970 Monte Carlo SS 454 is one of 3,823 built; another 1,919 rolled out in 1971.

Standard power for the 1970 SS 454 Monte Carlo
was the Chevelle's 360 horsepower LS5 454.
Compression was 10.25:1 and maximum torque
was 500lb-ft at 3200rpm.

Chapter 4

A Breed Above
Camaro: Chevrolet's Pony Car

In August 1964, General Motors officials gave the go-ahead for the F-car project, Chevrolet's response to Ford's pony car progenitor, the Mustang. Chevy's F-body Camaro, introduced on September 29, 1966, hit the ground running, making up more than two years of lost time in short order.

Initially, the hot Camaro package featured the ever-present Super Sport option group, which included the 295 horsepower 350 cubic inch small-block, a special hood with simulated air intakes, an accent stripe on the nose, SS badging, and wide-oval red-stripe rubber. The original Camaro SS was a certified eye-catcher, but no match for Ford's potent big-block GT Mustang. Chevrolet solved this problem in November 1966 when the big-block 396 Mk IV V-8 was made an optional Super Sport power source—first in 325 horsepower trim, followed later by the 375 horsepower L78 version.

Yet another impressive introduction came in November 1966, this one for the legendary Z/28, intended to homologate the Camaro platform for competition in Sports Car Club of America (SCCA) Trans-Am competition. The Z/28's 302 cubic inch V-8, one of Detroit's hottest small-blocks, was created by installing the 283's crankshaft in a 327 block. This ploy allowed Chevy to stay within SCCA racing's 305 cubic inch legal limit. Conservatively rated at 290 horsepower, Chevy's hybrid small-block was described by *Car and Driver* as "the most responsive American V-8 we've ever tested."

A revised accent stripe up front represented the most noticeable Camaro SS change for 1968. Rally Sport options for 1968 totalled 40,977; Super Sport production was 27,884. Note the restyled Rally wheel with its large center cap, again a feature included with the optional front disc brakes. In 1968, SS 396 Camaro buyers could choose from three big-block V-8s, as the 325 horsepower and 375 horsepower 396s were joined by a 350 horsepower version.

The 302 would remain the heart and soul of the Z/28 through 1969.

F-body news for 1968 included recognizable exterior emblems for the Z/28 and two additional 396 big-blocks. The 350 horsepower 396 joined the 325- and 375-horse versions on the SS equipment list, as did the rarely seen L89 aluminum head option for the L78 396. Retaining the L78's 375 horsepower rating, the L89 option simply lightened the load for race-minded customers.

Revised sheet metal helped make the

Priced at $210, the Super Sport package for the 1967 Camaro featured a distinctive accent stripe up front, fake air inlets on the hood, "SS" badging, and a 295 horsepower 350 cubic inch small-block V-8. Later in the year, the nose stripe would become an option for all Camaros. This 1967 SS convertible also features the Rally Sport equipment group, which added hideaway headlights. The mag-style wheel covers were optional. Camaro SS production for 1967, coupes and convertibles, totaled 34,411. RS convertibles numbered 10,675.

exceptionally stylish 1969 Camaro perhaps the most popular edition of Chevy's long-running F-body pony car performance package. Power options were basically unchanged with one major exception—the exotic ZL1 427. Featuring an aluminum block and heads, the race-ready ZL1 was created using the Central Office Production Order system, a quick way to cut corporate red tape, as well as avoid upper office roadblocks. COPO ZL1 Camaros were brutally fast, scorching the quarter-mile in nearly 13 seconds flat. Chevy performance guru Vince Piggins and Illinois Chevrolet dealer Fred Gibb put their heads together and used COPOs to build fifty ZL1 Camaros for Gibbs' lot in La Harpe, Illinois. Another nineteen COPO 9560 ZL1 Camaros were built for various other dealers across the country.

Another Chevy dealer, Don Yenko of Canonsburg, Pennsylvania, turned to Piggins and his COPO pipeline in 1969 to supply Yenko Chevrolet with factory-built 427 Camaros which he would then convert into Yenko Super Cars. Listed under COPO 9561, the L72 425 horsepower cast-iron 427 Camaro became the base for the 1969 Yenko Camaro, a high-powered hybrid capable of low 13-second quarters.

A stunning restyle shaped the Camaro image for 1970. For the first time, the Z/28 package was not powered by the 302, a variation of the Corvette's hot 360 horsepower LT1 350 cubic inch small-block taking its place. More of an off-the-line warrior, the 1970-1/2 Z/28 offered quarter-mile performance in the low 14-second range.

Listed under RPO L48, the Camaro Super Sport's 295 horsepower 350 featured 10.25:1 compression, hydraulic lifters, and forged steel rods and crank. With a few minor tuning tricks, courtesy of performance dealer Bill Thomas, *Hot Rod* managed a best quarter-mile run of 14.85 seconds at 95.65mph in a 1967 L48 SS Camaro. *Car and Driver's* results were considerably slower at 16.1 seconds 87mph.

A good ZL-1 . . . would produce somewhere in excess of 500hp without any attention to detail whatsoever.
—Tom Langdon in *Chevrolet Big-Block Muscle Cars*

Left
The SS package's price jumped to $263 when the L35 325 horsepower 396 big-block was announced as a Camaro Super Sport power choice early in the 1967 model run. The attractive Rally wheels on this Rally Sport SS 396 Camaro signify the presence of the optional front disc brakes. The vented 14in Rally rims were included with the RPO J52 front discs.

Rated at 325 horsepower, RPO L35 was the base 396 big-block for the 1967 SS Camaro. The hotter 375 horsepower L78 396 waited in the wings, but the cost of admission was nearly double that of the L35. The impressive 375 horsepower 396 featured a durable four-bolt main bearing block, while the 325 horsepower L35 had two-bolt mains.

Left
Fifteen-inch Corvette Rally rims and contrasting hood stripes represented the only exterior identification for Chevrolet's first Z/28 Camaro, introduced November 29, 1966, at Riverside International Raceway in California. The legendary Z/28 fender badges wouldn't come until March 1968. Z/28 equipment included front disc brakes, F41 sport suspension, quick-ratio steering, 3.73:1 gears, a Muncie four-speed, and the sensational 302 cubic inch small-block. Only 602 Z/28s were built for 1967.

The Z/28's hybrid 302 was conservatively rated at 290 horsepower and featured 11:1 compression, a hot solid-lifter cam, L79 327 heads with big valves, transistorized ignition, and an 800cfm Holley four-barrel on an aluminum intake. Modeled after NASCAR racing induction tricks designed by Smokey Yunick, the cowl induction air cleaner was a $79 option delivered in a Z/28's trunk to be installed by the dealer.

Previous pages
Chevy performance proponent Vince Piggins first suggested building the Z/28 in August 1966 to homologate the package for SCCA Trans-Am competition, where Mustangs and Plymouth Barracudas would be the Camaro's main rivals. Piggins' first choice for the car's name was "Cheetah," but in the end it was the optional group's RPO number that got the nod. Little known in its first year, the Z/28 jumped considerably in popularity for 1968, reaching sales of 7,199, followed by 19,014 in 1969.

Although the Z/28 Camaro was better suited for race action at the track, it could be equipped with all Camaro luxury and convenience options, including the Rally Sport package with its hideaway headlights. Here, this uncommonly plush 1967 Z/28 interior includes optional deluxe Parchment appointments, the sporty center console and gauge cluster.

With solid lifters and 11:1 compression, the L78 375 horsepower 396 was clearly meant for some serious action. When backed by a Muncie four-speed and 3.31:1 positraction gears, an L78 SS 396 Camaro could easily run the quarter-mile in the 14-second range. Special-duty differentials with stump-pulling ratios like 4.10:1, 4.56:1, and 4.88:1 promised even more.

Left
Race-minded Chevy dealer Don Yenko first began transplanting 427s into Camaros at his Canonsburg, Pennsylvania, facility in 1967. In 1969, he ordered a special run of COPO 9561 F-bodies—Camaros equipped with 425 horsepower Corvette 427s. Distinctive Yenko graphics and badges, 427 emblems, and a choice between the standard COPO equipment 15in Rally rims or optional Atlas five-spoke mags were part of the Yenko package.

Although some minor confusion exists concerning exactly how many 1969 Yenko Camaro SCs were built, the widely accepted—and presently documented—figure is 201. COPO 9561 L72 Camaros were also sold by Chevrolet, with 1,015 425 horsepower 427 V-8s produced for F-body applications in 1969. The ZL2 air induction hood was a standard COPO 9561 feature, while the "Yenko/SC" striping and 427 badges were installed at Canonsburg. This SC's vinyl roof was a factory option.

The big news isn't the gauges . . . it's what the gauges are connected to!

—1966 Chevrolet advertisement

The L72 427 lurking beneath a Yenko Camaro hood featured a cast-iron block and heads and an advertised 450 horsepower. An 800cfm Holley four-barrel fed the beast, a solid-lifter cam helped deliver the juice, and 11:1 pistons squeezed the mixture. Backed by an M21 Muncie four-speed and standard 4.10:1 positraction gears, the L72 transformed a Camaro into a quarter-mile terror— 12.80 at 108mph off the lot with street rubber and optional Doug Thorley headers, according to *Super Stock & Drag Illustrated's* Ro McGonegal. Slicks and tuning tricks lowered those figures even further to an astonishing 12.10 seconds at 114mph.

All 1969 Yenko models, Camaro or Chevelle, got custom headrest covers featuring the "sYc" logo for Yenko Super Car. Joining the 201 Yenko Camaros in 1969 were another ninety-nine similarly bedecked 427 Yenko Chevelle SCs.

Conservatively rated at 430 horsepower, the 12:1 compression ZL1 427 easily put out more than 500 horses, demonstrated by its ability to run the quarter in nearly 13 seconds flat. ZL1 427 features included an iron-sleeved aluminum block and open chamber aluminum heads, along with an aluminum bellhousing and transmission case. These helped keep engine weight down in the 500 pound range; a ZL1 big-block weighed no more than a small-block V-8.

Right
Other than the ZL2 air induction hood, no exterior clues give away the identity of an awesome 1969 ZL1 427 COPO 9560 Camaro. Along with that hood and the 430 horsepower all-aluminum 427, COPO 9560 equipment also included a heavy-duty Harrison radiator, transistorized ignition, special suspension, and a 14-bolt rear end. Mandatory options included front disc brakes and a choice between M21 or M22 "Rock Crusher" Muncie four-speeds and the Turbo-Hydramatic 400 automatic. Typical ZL1 stickered at nearly $7,300. Only sixty-nine were built.

Chapter 5

America's Sports Car
Classic Corvettes

Forty years and a million models after it first set rubber on American roads, Chevrolet's Corvette remains as this country's premier sports car. This achievement shouldn't be dimmed by the fact that it has basically reigned for four decades as this country's *only* sports car. Pretenders to the throne have been few, and save for Carroll Shelby's uncivilized Cobra, itself a match only as far as sheer brute force was concerned, the Corvette has remained unequalled .

Beginnings, however, were humble. The first-edition 1953–1955 Corvette was somewhat awkward and weakly-received; the public considered it more of a curiosity than anything. Insufficient market interest almost cancelled Harley Earl's 'glass-bodied baby in 1954, but V-8 power saved it the following year. Zora Arkus-Duntov's growing involvement with the car also helped to turn things around. By 1956 Chevrolet had itself a winner. A startling restyle, combined with some serious

performance engineering courtesy of Duntov, put the 1956 Corvette on the right track. Armed with two four-barrel carburetors, the 1955 Corvette's polite 265 cubic inch V-8 was transformed into 1956's 255 horsepower bully.

Fuel injection debuted in 1957, landing the Corvette's enlarged 283 cubic inch small-block into the newly created "one-horsepower-per-cubic-inch" club (Chrysler had broken the barrier the year before with the 300B's 355 horsepower 354 cubic inch hemi). Although early

Optional side exhausts and standard four-wheel disc brakes debuted in 1965, but the really big news came up front in the form of the Corvette's first big-block, the 396 cubic inch Mk IV V-8. The 396 Mk IV, nicknamed "porcupine head" for its canted-valve design, was a direct descendant of the 427 cubic inch Mk II engine that shook the NASCAR troops at Daytona just as GM was closing the door on factory racing activities in February 1963. A special bulging hood was included when the 396 Turbo-Jet was ordered.

Chevrolet's fiberglass Corvette two-seater was offered only in Polo White when introduced in 1953. Three additional shades were added in 1954: Pennant Blue, Sportsman Red, and black. In all, 3,640 1954 Corvettes were built, less than one-third of Chevy's projected total. Opinions varied concerning styling and performance. But even though the car's creator, Zora Arkus-Duntov, wasn't happy with the 1953–1954 Corvette's performance, handling and acceleration were above average by American standards of the time; 0–60mph took 11 seconds, and the car topped out at 105mph.

versions of the injected V-8 were often disagreeable and difficult to maintain, it would remain as the top Corvette performance option through 1965. The 327 was the last fuel-injected Corvette engine of the 1960s, achieving a maximum output rating of 375 horsepower before it was displaced by the brutish 396 cubic inch Mk IV big-block V-8 in 1966.

Partial restyles in 1958 and 1960 freshened the Corvette's face, but paled in comparison to 1963's makeover. The body was Bill Mitchell's idea, with final lines penned by Larry Shinoda. Looking an awful lot like Mitchell's Stingray racer of 1959, the all-new Corvette Sting Ray was as innovative underneath as it was stunning on top, thanks to Duntov's devotion to

Powering the 1953, 1954, and early 1955 Corvettes was Chevrolet's 235 cubic inch Blue Flame six-cylinder, based on the same "Stovebolt" six that served more mundane duty under standard passenger car hoods. As a Corvette powerplant, the 235 six featured three Carter carbs, a relatively radical high-lift cam, 8:1 compression, and a split exhaust manifold feeding dual exhausts. Maximum output was 150 horsepower at 4200rpm. This 1954 Blue Flame six uses twin air cleaners in place of the three "bullet-type" breathers installed in 1953. Complete chrome dress-up was also available for these engines.

Looking much sleeker, the second-generation 1956–1957 Corvette was not only more popular than its predecessor but also more civilized, with the addition of roll-up windows and a removable hardtop. Performance improvements included **various chassis updates to improve handling and optional twin four-barrel carburetors in 1956, followed by fuel injection in 1957. This black beauty is one of 6,339 Corvettes built for 1957; 1956 production was 3,467.**

independent rear suspension. In reference to the 1963 Sting Ray, Duntov told *Car and Driver*, "I now have a Corvette I can be proud to drive in Europe." Offered both as Corvette's first coupe rendition, as well as in typical topless fashion, Shinoda's timeless Sting Ray shape lasted through five model runs, and

many feel the Corvette was never better.

Performance enhancements during the span included the aforementioned big-block introduction for 1965, a powerful package that was pumped up to 427 cubic inches in 1966. The awesome aluminum head L88 option for the 427 appeared in 1967, followed by the

In 1957, engineers bored out the Corvette's small-block V-8 to 283 cubic inches and upped the output ante to one horsepower per cubic inch with the optional Ramjet fuel injection setup. Actually, the Ramjet option was available in two forms, the 283 horsepower version with 10.5:1 compression and the 250 horsepower 283 fuelie with a 9.5:1 ratio. Also new for 1957 was a four-speed manual transmission. According to *Road & Track*, a four-speed 283 horsepower fuelie Corvette could go 0–60mph in 5.7 seconds. Quarter-mile time for the same car was a sizzling 14.3 seconds.

ultimate big-block Vette, 1969's all-aluminum 427 ZL1.

Meanwhile, Mitchell and Shinoda had turned out another new Corvette look for 1968. Featuring what would become General Motors' familiar "Coke-bottle" body, the fifth generation Corvette was, in *Car and Driver's* opinion, "the best yet."

In 1970, the optional 370 horsepower LT1 350 cubic inch V-8 appeared, balancing the brutish big-block boulevard Vettes—which had reached their pinnacle that same year in LS5 454 cubic inch form—with a well-rounded agile road rocket. Not since the fuel-injected 327 had disappeared after 1965 had Corvette buyers been able to combine serious small-block power with a well-balanced, road-hugging stance. The LT1 small-block and 454 big-block carried the Corvette banner high into Detroit's post-performance years—the LT1 falling by the wayside after 1972, and the 454 doing the same two years later.

Left
The last of the solid-axle Corvettes, the 1962 model foretold the coming of the classic Sting Ray in 1963 through its boat-tail rear, which had first appeared in 1961. Although its grille was devoid of the earlier models' teeth, the 1962 Corvette's quad headlight front end was a direct descendant of the design introduced for 1958. Top performance option in 1962 was the 360 horsepower fuel-injected 327 cubic inch V-8. Total 1962 Corvette production was 14,531.

The Corvette's 283 cubic inch V-8 was bored and stroked to 327 cubic inches for 1962. In basic tune, the 1962 Corvette 327 was rated at 250 horsepower. Three other 327s were available, the 300- and 340-horse carbureted small-blocks and the king-of-the-hill 360 horsepower fuel-injected version.

Sports cars are by their nature controversial: they arouse the interest of the adolescent— and of those reaching second childhood.

—Roy Lunn, SAE paper 611F
in *American Muscle*

Befitting its name, the totally restyled 1963 Corvette Sting Ray featured its own "stinger," a spine that ran the length of the car; it began as a center bulge on the hood, and ended in this split window design on the coupe model's boat-tail rear. Duntov didn't like the idea, nor did drivers who preferred seeing what they were about to back over. But Bill Mitchell insisted the split window theme remain, which it did for one year only.

A serious performance powerplant with solid lifters and 11:1 compression, the 1965 Corvette's 396 Turbo-Jet produced maximum power of 425 horsepower at 6400rpm. Maximum torque was 415lb-ft at 4000rpm. All this brute force translated into a 0–60mph time of 5.7 seconds and quarter-mile performance of 14.1 seconds at 103mph. Reported top end for a 1965 396 Corvette was 136mph.

Left

In 1966, the 396 Turbo-Jet became the 427 Turbo-Jet, available in 390- and 425-horse forms. A triple-carb option in 1967 pumped up output to 435 horsepower, but the most potent Corvette power choice that year was actually advertised at five fewer horses. Given a 430 horsepower factory rating, the rare L88 427 probably put out somewhere between 500 and 600 real horses. Only 20 L88 Corvettes were produced for 1967.

Obviously built for racing, L88 427 features included aluminum heads, beefy internals, a 0.540/0.560 solid-lifter cam, 12.5:1 compression, a huge 830cfm Holley four-barrel, and an open-element air cleaner. Knowing a racer would quickly replace it anyway, the L88's exhaust system remained typical stock Corvette hardware. Backing up the L88 was a 10.5in heavy-duty clutch and a lightweight nodular iron flywheel.

In 1969, the awesome L88 Corvette was superseded by the outrageous ZL1, an all-aluminum 427 also laughably rated at 430 horsepower. Again, actual output was more like 560 horsepower, but who was counting? Factory numbers games mattered little once behind the wheel of a ZL1 Corvette. Press tests put performance at a shocking 12.1 seconds through the quarter-mile, topping out at 116mph. Of course, that much speed didn't come cheap; the ZL1 option cost around $3,000. Only two were built.

Weighing some 100lb less than the aluminum-head L88, the ZL1 kept its weight down by using an iron-sleeved aluminum cylinder block. Everything the L88 was, the ZL1 did one better. Internals were even beefier, and a modified solid-lifter cam featuring revised ramp profiles was included, as were big-valve, open chamber aluminum cylinder heads. Compression remained the same, but pistons were reinforced.

In contrast to the brutal big-block Corvettes, the LT1-equipped models, introduced in 1970, were well-balanced performers; agile as well as muscular, they took many enthusiasts back to the fuelie's days when Corvettes were more sports car and less quarter-mile warrior. For 1970, the hot 350 cubic inch LT1 small-block was rated at 370 horsepower. In 1971 that rating dropped to 330 horsepower, and the final rendition was advertised at 255 net horses. This 1972 LT1 Corvette is one of 1,741 built. Production in 1970 and 1971 was 1,287 and 1,949, respectively. All LT1s got a distinctive hood modeled after the 1968–1969 L88/ZL1 design.

Index